TURNING POINTS

THE END OF THE
COLD WAR

BY KATE RIGGS

CREATIVE EDUCATION • CREATIVE PAPERBACKS

Published by Creative Education and Creative Paperbacks
P.O. Box 227, Mankato, Minnesota 56002
Creative Education and Creative Paperbacks are imprints of
The Creative Company
www.thecreativecompany.us

Design and production by The Design Lab
Art direction by Rita Marshall
Printed in China

Photographs by Corbis (Bettmann, CORBIS, The Dmitri Baltermants
Collection, Owen Franken, Douglas Kirkland, Todd Korol/Aurora Photos,
Wally McNamee), Getty Images (China Photos, FPG, Getty Images, Ronald
L. Haeberle/Time Life Pictures, Hulton Archive, Keystone, LUBOMIR KOTEK,
Laski Diffusion, Walter Sanders, Charles E. Steinheimer/Time Life Pictures, Tom
Stoddart Archive, Julian Wasser/Time Life Pictures)

Library of Congress Cataloging-in-Publication Data

Riggs, Kate.
The end of the Cold War / Kate Riggs.
p. cm. — (Turning points)
Includes bibliographical references and index.
Summary: A historical account of the end of the Cold War, including the events
that sparked conflict and led to peace, the competition for global ideological
supremacy, and the lingering aftermath.

ISBN 978-1-60818-748-5 (hardcover)
ISBN 978-1-62832-344-3 (pbk)
ISBN 978-1-56660-783-4 (eBook)
Cold War—Juvenile literature. / World politics—1945–1989—Juvenile literature.

D843.R515 2016
909.82/5—dc23   2016000992

CCSS: RI.5.1, 2, 3, 8; RI. 6.1, 2, 4, 7; RH.6-8.3, 4, 5, 6, 7, 8

First Edition HC 9 8 7 6 5 4 3 2 1
First Edition PBK 9 8 7 6 5 4 3 2 1

Cover, main image: A 1957 test of an atomic bomb
This page: 1960s American schoolchildren practicing "duck and cover" drills

TABLE *of* CONTENTS

INTRODUCTION

A wall can be a stabilizing force. Or it can be a barrier. During the Cold War, the Berlin Wall was a barrier. It physically separated the eastern and western sectors of the German city of Berlin. It also became symbolic of the division between East and West. The East consisted of the **Soviet Union** and its **communist** partners. The West was represented by the United States and its non-communist allies. Although Berlin had been divided into four parts in 1945, it wasn't until 1961 that a wall went up.

In November 1989, thousands of Berliners peacefully gathered at the wall to celebrate the newly opened passage.

In the meantime, the Soviets spent years trying to prevent people from leaving East Germany via West Berlin. From June to mid-August 1961, some 67,000 fled communist control and poor living conditions. On August 13, 1961, the East German government closed the border between East and West Berlin. The wall began with barbed wire and wooden sawhorses. Within a year, the makeshift wall was eight feet (2.4 m) high. It eventually grew to 12 feet (3.7 m) of reinforced concrete. On the East German side, floodlights shone on the sand near the base. Soldiers patrolled, and dogs were trained to attack.

On November 9, 1989, that Wall was dismantled. Soviet republics soon declared their independence. Free elections were held. By December 8, 1991, the Soviet Union was no more. The world had turned sharply from the depths of the Cold War into an uncertain future.

Although the Polish city of Warsaw had once been magnificent, by the end of World War II, more than 85 percent of its buildings had been destroyed.

DRAWING THE CURTAIN

Why had the Berlin Wall gone up in the first place, though? To understand that, first consider what the world was like at the end of World War II. European cities were piles of stones and shards of glass. More than 50 million people had been killed. The Soviet Union alone had lost 27 million. Most of those killed in action were young adults of working age. Battles had been fought in forests, along rivers, and inside homes and businesses. In six years, much of the continent had been bombed past recognition. The entire world was weary. Former **colonial** powers such as Great Britain and France suffered additional losses abroad. Winning the war had come at a devastating cost. The Soviets, especially, expected to be repaid by the other Allies for their vast sacrifice.

In the U.S., whose mainland had been more haven than battleground, conditions were much better. Industry was stronger than ever, thanks to the "war effort" of making parts for machines and weapons. The U.S. had contributed many planes, warships, and other militaristic needs. After

Once war-rationing restrictions ended in 1945, new vehicles were in high demand, causing American manufacturers to produce record numbers of vehicles.

the war, it was one of the only places capable of continuing such heavy manufacturing. In 1946 alone, the U.S. produced 2 million cars.

The U.S. was not the only part of the Americas that was fit to serve others. South American countries that had supported the Allies were also primed for more industrialization. Because of certain trade agreements, many South American resources were already funneled to the U.S. by 1941. Trade relationships soon became stronger in the Americas. It was more difficult for Britain, France, and Germany to get goods then.

When Germany invaded the Soviet Union in 1941, it took the country by surprise. Adolf Hitler and Joseph Stalin had agreed not to fight two years before. What's more, the Soviets supplied Germany with grain and materials such as rubber. This kept the German army well stocked. In fact, it enabled Germany to stage the invasion! More than 32,000 Soviet factories, 100,000 farms, and 71,000 entire towns and villages were then destroyed.

As the East and West vied for control after World War II, young East Berliners paraded with a sign that declared Stalin to be "the best friend of the German people."

Stalin's desire to create a buffer zone to avoid future invasions started with his annexation of eastern Germany. With the help of propaganda and removal of political opponents, the Soviets soon installed communist governments throughout Eastern Europe. Countries such as Poland, Romania, Bulgaria, and Hungary became pro-Soviet within two years of the war's end.

This made the West anxious. Communist governments seemed much less stable than democratic ones. And they were usually led by charismatic, powerful dictators who did not always deal fairly with international partners—or their own people. Although Marxism eschewed the power of individual leaders, it was the cult of personality developed by each Soviet leader that affected the actions of the nation as a whole.

Joseph Stalin

Stalin's motives were even more complicated than his predecessors'. For Stalin, spreading communism was akin to expanding the historical kingdom of Russia. And he identified strongly with the powerful kings of Russia's heyday such as Peter the Great. Stalin also did not trust the motives of Western nations—and he did not wish to be stopped. He did not appreciate any form of political opposition, and the Soviet people knew this firsthand. With all they had suffered during World War II, their postwar experience was not much better.

The U.S. objective early on was to "contain" Soviet influence to Eastern Europe. The Truman

POINTING OUT

STALIN'S REIGN OF TERROR

Joseph Stalin was notorious for his dislike of opposition. But he took it to a terrifying level. Stalin's rise within the Communist Party involved getting rid of his competitors. At first, this simply meant throwing people out of the party. Between 1936 and 1938, though, Stalin used the police force to target senior party leaders, the army, and then the entire country. This period, known as the "Great Purge," resulted in mass arrests and executions. Millions were sent to labor camps or killed in prisons. Stalin would be the uncontested dictator until his death in 1953.

In the 1930s, Stalin's dictatorship caused Russians to turn against each other; here, mechanical workers vote to punish the counter-revolutionaries among them.

HUAC interviewed numerous celebrities, such as Lucille Ball, under suspicion of being communist sympathizers.

Doctrine became the primary policy by which the U.S. enacted this goal. Named after president Harry Truman, the policy was "to support free peoples who are resisting attempted subjugation by armed minorities or by outside pressures." It was impossible for Truman to consider that all that had been done to end World War II could potentially be undone by communism. Now that the U.S. was actively involved on a global stage, there would be no going back. The country was invested in helping other nations. And it was in a uniquely powerful position to do so in the late 1940s.

To Western eyes, Stalin's tactics looked suspiciously similar to Hitler's. It became increasingly evident that dividing lines were being drawn. As former British prime minister Winston Churchill described it in a 1946 speech, "From Stettin in the Baltic to Trieste in the Adriatic, an iron curtain has descended across the Continent. Behind that line lie all the capitals of the ancient states of Central and Eastern Europe. Warsaw, Berlin, Prague, Vienna, Budapest, Belgrade, Bucharest and Sofia, all these famous cities and the populations around them lie in what I must call the Soviet sphere, and all are subject in one form or another, not only to Soviet influence but to a very high and, in some cases, increasing measure of control from Moscow."

Berlin became an early battleground for Western vs. Soviet influence. The West attempted to initiate reforms that would empower the German economy, making it align with its own **capitalist** systems. In 1948, the Soviets blockaded West Berlin, cutting off transportation routes by road and canal. But the Western allies airlifted food and supplies for almost a year, unwilling to give the entire city over to the Soviets. When the blockade ended on May 12, 1949, the U.S. was seen as the victor over Soviet "aggression." Later that month, the republic of West Germany was established. (East Germany began functioning as a state in October 1949.)

By August, though, the Soviet Union scored a major point. It tested its first atomic weapon. When the U.S. was developing atomic bombs during World War II, spies had shared secrets with the Soviets. That intelligence paid off. Suddenly, the U.S. and Soviet Union were on a completely different playing field. Both countries having nuclear capabilities was a threat the world had never seen. With weapons in play that could unleash even more terrible horrors, the Cold War of the 1950s became one of hot potential.

At the peak of "Operation Vittles," an aircraft landed every 45 seconds, delivering food and fuel to West Berliners.

During the 1953 operation known as Upshot-Knothole, the U.S. conducted 11 test shots of nuclear warheads over a 12-week period.

CHAPTER TWO

A WORLD IN CRISIS

As the U.S. and Soviet Union tried to deter each other from having to use those nuclear weapons, the conflict escalated. Over the course of the Cold War, the two countries spent an estimated combined total of $8 trillion on weapons development. The idea was that, by one-upping each other, nuclear war could be prevented. Because no one wanted to actually start a war that would end in mutual catastrophe. However, this strategy may have lengthened the conflict instead: there was no clear end in sight. And who would come out the winner under such circumstances?

The U.S. focused increasingly on stopping communism. Sometimes it backed **repressive** leaders just to prevent communism from gaining a foothold. As Richard Ned Lebow and Janice Gross Stein note in their book, *We All Lost the Cold War*, "In South Korea, southern Africa, Chile, Central America, and the Caribbean, Democratic and Republican administrations alike kept corrupt governments in power. By the end of the Cold War, the U.S. was widely regarded as a powerful obstacle to democratic change." For the U.S. to flip from a symbol of freedom and justice in 1945 to an "obstacle" by 1991, something drastic must have taken place.

That something was the extreme paranoia of the Cold War. And it wasn't a feeling without basis. Like the territories occupied by Nazi Germany, the areas previously controlled by Japan were divvied up among the Allies in 1945. The northern half of the Korean **peninsula** was given to the Soviets. The southern half went to the U.S. On June 25, 1950, North Korea invaded the democratic republic of South Korea. The first American troops were sent to support the South Koreans the following month. China and the Soviet Union backed North Korea. The fear was that the Korean War could grow into a direct confrontation between the U.S. and China/the Soviet Union. It was also an issue of containing communism. "If we let Korea down," president Harry Truman said, "the Soviet[s] will keep right on going and swallow up one [place] after another."

In July 1953, all the sides agreed to bring the Korean War to a close. Not long after that, though, another conflict emerged. Also in Southeast Asia, this time the flashpoint was Vietnam. A former French colony, Vietnam threw off French rule in 1954. Communist leader Ho Chi Minh was granted control over North Vietnam. Former Vietnamese emperor Bao Dai remained in South Vietnam as its chief of state. When he was voted out of office in 1955, the anti-communist Ngo Dinh Diem took over as president. This set up a showdown with North Vietnam. American president Dwight Eisenhower pledged support to Diem.

Under **Nikita Khrushchev**, the Soviet Union was not as active in supporting Ho Chi Minh—at

President Truman's signing of the European Recovery Act of 1948 (or the Marshall Plan) allowed for $13.3 billion of economic aid to be released to western European countries.

Though Khrushchev and Mao appeared amiable in public, the communist leaders privately attempted to undermine each other as they argued over borders and resources.

first. It wanted to avoid escalating the crisis with the U.S. However, China and its communist leader, Mao Zedong, did not necessarily share the same concerns. For China, it was more important to weaken the positions of both the Soviets and the Americans. Although Mao had been a great friend of Stalin's, he was not taken with Khrushchev. This new Soviet leader was much more emotional and more concerned with reforming within his own country. To Khrushchev, Stalin was a tyrannical traitor to the communist party. As he wrote in his memoirs, "Stalin called everyone who didn't agree with him an 'enemy of the people.'… As a result, several hundred thousand honest people perished. Everyone lived in fear in those days. Everyone expected that at any moment there would be a knock on the door in the middle of the night and that knock on the door would prove fatal.… [P]eople not to Stalin's liking were annihilated, honest party members, irreproachable people, loyal and hard workers for our cause who had gone through the school of revolutionary struggle under Lenin's leadership. This was utter and complete arbitrariness. And now is all this to be forgiven and forgotten? Never!"

Rather than provoking the U.S. directly, Khrushchev concentrated on expanding Soviet missile and space technology in the late 1950s. Soviet breakthroughs (or boasting of them) in these

At the 1958 World's Fair in Brussels, Belgium, the Soviet Union displayed its latest technological achievements, including a replica of Sputnik 1.

POINTING OUT

SPUTNIK AND THE SPACE RACE

Once the Soviet Union successfully launched Sputnik 1, *the "space race" with the U.S. was on. The Soviets were clearly ahead of the game at the beginning. They sent another satellite into orbit in November 1957. This one carried a dog. It took the Americans until January 31, 1958, to get their first craft aloft. The Soviets answered by sending an unmanned spacecraft around the moon in October 1959. Then the first person to travel in space was Yuri Gagarin, in April 1961. The U.S. didn't achieve a true "first" until July 20, 1969. That was the day Apollo 11 landed on the moon.*

arenas then, of course, had the effect of provoking Americans. The U.S., thanks to its U-2 spy planes, was able to gather the first reliable photographic evidence of Soviet weapons capabilities in August 1960. What it discovered was that the arsenal was nowhere near as large as previously thought. In fact, it was about half the size of America's nuclear stronghold. For years, Americans had been led to believe the U.S. was critically behind and should ramp up weapons production.

Much of that arms race was brought about by miscalculation and early ordering on America's part. Because it took several years to produce and obtain the type of long-range missiles supposedly needed to battle the Soviets, the U.S. operated

East German workers and soldiers fortified the 96-mile-long (155 km) Berlin Wall with glass shards, barbed wire, and guard towers.

on an *estimation* of Soviet capabilities seven years down the line. Weapons were then purchased to match that rough number. The "strategic buildup" effectively caused more problems and proved to be a poor strategy. Once new president John F. Kennedy learned of this in 1961, weapons production temporarily took a backseat to other concerns. That was the year the Berlin Wall went up. A few months before the Wall, a disaster happened in Cuba.

In April 1961, the Central Intelligence Agency (CIA) led a mission to invade Cuba. Their objective was to overthrow the communist government of **Fidel Castro**. The plan did not work. After three days, Castro's forces defeated and imprisoned the invaders. The Bay of Pigs disaster became the Kennedy administration's "'political Achilles' heel'"—Kennedy became obsessed with avenging it but could not overthrow Castro by direct militaristic means. Khrushchev took the opportunity to strengthen Soviet ties to Cuba. He and Castro then began to use the small island nation as a staging ground for Soviet missiles.

This was done in secret, though. In the end, it seemed as though Khrushchev wanted to scare Americans. Perhaps he wanted them to feel what the Soviets felt after the Americans placed Jupiter missiles on their doorsteps in Turkey. (The missiles were within range of Moscow.) Intimidation tactics employed by both Khrushchev and Kennedy unintentionally caused the type of confrontation both leaders were trying to avoid. For 13 days in October 1962, the world came close to witnessing a nuclear war. If the U.S. had ordered a strike on Moscow, the missiles in Cuba could have been used against cities in the southeastern U.S. Khrushchev later revealed that they were targeted to do so.

POINTING OUT

THE SPY WHO SAVED THE WORLD

*Oleg Penkovsky was a colonel in the Soviet intelligence agency known as GRU. In December 1960, he became a **mole** for the U.S. and Britain. Equipped with a miniature camera, he photographed hundreds of Soviet documents. He also informed American intelligence that the missiles in Cuba were incapable of launching accurately, according to what he knew of Soviet tech at the time. Such assurance backed President Kennedy's stance during the 1962 crisis. Afterward, Penkovsky paid a high price for his help. The Soviets arrested Penkovsky as a suspected spy. He was killed in May 1963.*

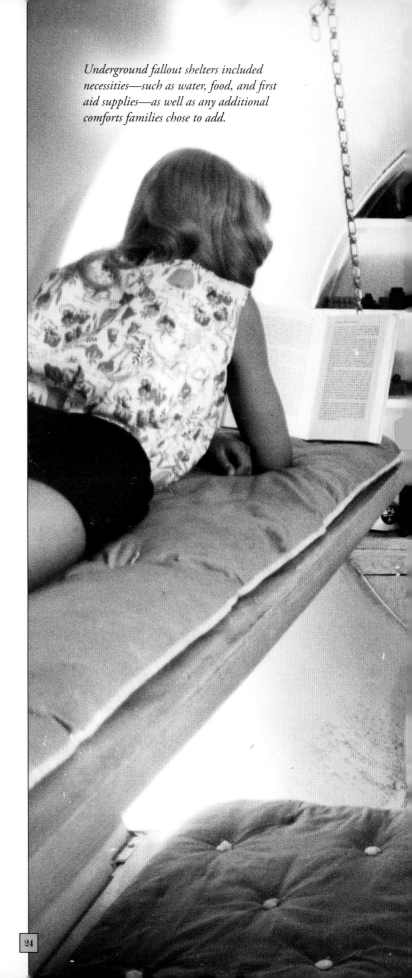

Underground fallout shelters included necessities—such as water, food, and first aid supplies—as well as any additional comforts families chose to add.

CHAPTER THREE

GETTING COLDER

With the Cuban Missile Crisis defused, Kennedy and Khrushchev proceeded with caution. Kennedy agreed to remove the missiles from Turkey. Khrushchev dismantled those in Cuba. Both remained convinced of the other's hostility. Yet neither had a clear picture of their true intentions. It became the most dangerous guessing game in history.

After President Kennedy was shot on November 22, 1963, former vice president Lyndon B. Johnson continued the administration's work and attitudes. This included maintaining the tense standoff with Khrushchev. As the fighting in Vietnam raged throughout the 1960s, the Soviet Union and U.S. avoided direct military action against each other. Containing communism was still the American goal. However, that objective ultimately failed in Vietnam. Attempts to deter the communists using force resulted in the deaths of more than 3 million people. In 1975, the entire country came under communist control.

Vietnam, 1968

On December 1, 1962, a cargo ship transported the nuclear warheads out of Cuba, reaching the Soviet Union almost three weeks later.

At an emergency special session in New York, the United Nations Security Council discussed how to effect a ceasefire in the Arab-Israeli War in the Middle East.

As the U.S. was drawing down its troops in Vietnam in 1973, another crisis ballooned. This time, it was in the Middle East. On October 6, Egypt and Syria attacked Israeli forces in the Sinai Peninsula and Golan Heights. (These were areas Israel had occupied since a war in 1967.) The Soviets supplied weapons to Egypt and Syria, while the U.S. supported Israel. Publicly, U.S. secretary of state Henry Kissinger worked with Soviet leader Leonid Brezhnev to find a solution to the Arab-Israeli War. But mixed messages were sent behind the scenes. It was difficult for the Americans and Soviets to assess the situation accurately when the Israelis were reporting one thing and the Arabs had the opposite view.

Soviet leader Leonid Brezhnev (left) and U.S. president Richard Nixon (right) signed treaties agreeing to limit the production of nuclear missiles.

Late at night on October 24, Brezhnev sent a message to president Richard Nixon. He wanted the U.S. and Soviet Union to agree to send troops to the Middle East to provide a resolution: "I will say it straight that if you find it impossible to act jointly with us in this matter, we should be faced with the necessity urgently to consider the question of taking appropriate steps unilaterally." Kissinger interpreted this as a threat. The lesson he had learned from the 1962 Missile Crisis was that such threats had to be challenged. The U.S. responded by alerting its nuclear forces of potential action. The defense readiness condition (DEFCON) was raised to level 3, meaning that the air force should be ready to move within 15 minutes. It was the highest level since 1962's DEFCON 2 alert for the air force's Strategic Air Command.

POINTING OUT

THE MIRACLE ON ICE

Competition between Americans and Soviets during the Cold War was not limited to politics. It extended to sporting events as well. Some of the most memorable matchups occurred during the Olympics. In the 1980 Winter Games held in Lake Placid, New York, a historic showdown took place on the men's hockey rink. The underdog U.S. team unexpectedly took on the perennial gold-winning Soviets in the medal round. As ABC sportscaster Al Michaels was calling the incredible puck-scrambling action of the remaining seconds, with the U.S. in the lead, he provided the game's memorable nickname: "Do you believe in miracles?! Yes!"

Despite obvious mutual distrust, the lines of communication remained open. A flurry of messages between Washington and Moscow continued over the next two days. Finally, on October 27, Nixon and Brezhnev reached consensus. They agreed to cooperate and help the Arabs and Israelis achieve a ceasefire. The U.S returned to normal DEFCON 5 status in the following days, and all-out nuclear war was once again avoided. What could explain such a relaxation in attitude?

Brezhnev was committed to the policy of **détente** for a long time. During Brezhnev's 18-year leadership, the Soviet Union signed several arms-control, security, and trade agreements. Such treaties

As the Soviet Union poured money into militaristic and technological advancements throughout the Cold War, its economy suffered and unemployment soared.

were designed to hold the superpowers in check. As Nixon and Brezhnev exchanged memos during the Arab-Israeli crisis, they both kept in mind the treaty they had signed in May 1972. Still, neither side was completely willing to back down. As he strove for looser relations with the West, Brezhnev also increased spending for the Soviet military.

By the time Mikhail Gorbachev came to power in 1985, détente had broken down. Plus, there were other priorities. Gorbachev did not want to continue the expensive arms race because the Soviet Union had already paid too high of an economic price. He also did not see any real threat of a U.S. attack. So there was no need to try to match the Americans missile for missile. When president Ronald Reagan began his **Strategic Defense Initiative** (SDI), though, that seemed to suggest the Soviets needed more arms instead.

It was then up to Gorbachev to convince Reagan of his sincerity. Instead of responding in kind by ramping up weapons production, Gorbachev withdrew forces from warzones. He freed Soviet political prisoners. He talked about much-needed reforms.

Soviet leaders had always seemed motivated to change their relationship with the West more out of economic concern at home than anything else: like Khrushchev, Gorbachev needed more people and money available to be able to develop the economy. Too much of their resources were devoted to militaristic goals. They weren't able to do enough at home. Especially during the Brezhnev era, the Soviet military was strengthened at the expense of living conditions for ordinary citizens.

It was time to challenge the idea that the West was the enemy. It was time to cooperate with the rest of the world. And the world was finally ready to work together. Governments were tired of the Cold War. Europe was tired of division. People everywhere supported more peaceful measures.

By the mid-1980s, Gorbachev's plans for restructuring and openness meant that the stage was finally set for reform. Revolts began in parts of Eastern Europe. Gorbachev would not commit Soviet help to squash those revolts. Unlike previous leaders, he was not willing to do anything in the name of advancing communism. In October 1986, Gorbachev and Reagan met in Reykjavik, Iceland. Gorbachev wanted both countries to cut their stocks of nuclear weapons in half. Reagan agreed that the nukes needed to go. So they came up with a plan to get rid of the stockpiles by the year 2000. However, what Reagan did not want to do was limit SDI. Part of that plan involved testing missiles in space. Gorbachev was opposed to that. So no agreement was reached then. But the door had been opened to further talks. The following December, the Intermediate-Range Nuclear Forces Treaty was signed. It was the

Mikhail Gorbachev (left), who was openly critical of his predecessors, worked with President Reagan (right) for more than two years on the Intermediate-Range Nuclear Forces Treaty.

Although demolition of the Berlin Wall didn't officially begin until the summer of 1990, individuals were chiseling away parts of the wall to keep as souvenirs well beforehand.

first agreement the U.S. and Soviets had made that *reduced* the number of nuclear weapons. It committed both countries to eliminating a total of 2,692 missile systems within 18 months of the treaty's start date (June 1, 1988).

By the fall of 1989, mass demonstrations in East Germany were progressing toward another change. Gorbachev visited East Berlin in October 1989. Only a month later, on November 9, 1989, the first domino fell as the Berlin Wall was dismantled. Then Germany was reunified. Other Eastern European countries rapidly turned from communism. Soviet republics soon declared their independence. Free elections were held. By the end of December 1991, the Soviet Union was no more.

POINTING OUT

REAGAN AND THE WALL

In June 1987, President Reagan gave a speech in West Berlin. He famously addressed Gorbachev, at one point telling him to "tear down this wall!" But would Gorbachev have heard Reagan's words? According to the Soviet press agency TASS, the speech had been "openly provocative," which would not have made a favorable impression in the Soviet Union. There was little press coverage of the speech at all, even in the West. Still, it was a curious tack for the president to take, considering that he and Gorbachev were in the midst of nuclear negotiations.

SEPARATE BUT UNEQUAL

The end of the Cold War saw dramatic changes in the makeup of the world. The U.S. thought it had won. After all, new democracies were springing up everywhere. Yet the decades of spending money on the arms race and numerous wars had taken a toll. America was hugely in debt. The total by 1989 had reached $2.6 trillion. The government would continue to operate with budgets financed by debt until 1998. Taxes on the American people had also risen. Especially by the 1980s, the U.S. focused so exclusively on the Cold War that other concerns fell to the side. **Infrastructure** suffered. Unemployment was high. Funding was not invested in public education or new technologies. Apart from economic effects, there were relational problems as well.

The international view of America was much changed. At the end of World War II, American soldiers were welcomed in war-torn countries. They were seen as enforcers of peace. The American way of life was attractive. Years of involvement in foreign conflicts had a negative effect, though. In its desire to contain communism, the U.S. had made many questionable alliances and decisions. Other countries were sometimes suspicious of U.S. interests.

As the Cold War drew to a close in the late 1980s, the rising rate of homelessness became an undeniable issue in many of America's major cities, such as Los Angeles.

Ten days after supporters of Václav Havel gathered in Prague's Wenceslas Square in 1989, he was elected Czechoslovakia's first noncommunist president in 40 years.

HAVEL

HAVEL NA HRAD

38

In the new Russian Federation, times were difficult. Before the Soviet Union had melted away, the first direct presidential election had put Boris Yeltsin in power. Yeltsin then brokered agreements with leaders of the Soviet republics to make them independent. The management of his own country proved to be much more challenging. Remaking Russia into a capitalist economy after nearly a century of being government-controlled was riddled with pitfalls. The sale of state-owned businesses to private parties meant job losses for many people: if no one wanted to buy the industry, people were out of work. Because communism had assigned certain parts of the country to certain industries, this was devastating. The government itself was in no better shape. It could not even collect taxes. So it wasn't able to pay state employees—including soldiers—for extended periods of time.

Similar stories of high unemployment and poorer living conditions were found throughout Eastern Europe in the 1990s. Yet some countries made the transition from communism to democracy relatively smoothly. In Czechoslovakia, the nonviolent Velvet Revolution in late 1989 paved the way for a peaceful transfer of power. By 1993, the country peacefully split itself into the Czech Republic and Slovakia. Neighbors to the southeast were not so fortunate.

Yugoslavia splintered apart in the early 1990s in a haze of violence. Traditionally, that area was home to several ethnic populations and a mix of religions. The major Slavic groups were Croat, Slovene, Serb, and Bosniak. Non-Slavic groups were in the minority. For centuries, all those peoples were moved and mixed around by occupying forces, from the Ottoman Empire to the Soviet state. Serbian politician Slobodan Milosevic stirred the pot in the

FIGHTING IN THE BALKANS

The Socialist Federal Republic of Yugoslavia included six republics during the Cold War. In 1991, Slovenia, Croatia, and Macedonia broke away from Yugoslavia. The following year, Serbia and Montenegro joined to become a new Yugoslavia. Bosnia and Herzegovina proclaimed its independence, and the Bosnian War would rage until late 1995. Ethnic divisions were at the heart of this conflict, as people of Serbian descent battled those of Croatian descent and Bosnian Muslims for control of the republic, supported (and armed) by Serbia and Croatia.

late 1980s. As the six republics split, one conflict after another broke out. The most disruptive was the Bosnian War, which began April 6, 1992. Serbs within Bosnia and Herzegovina revolted with the help of Milosevic and the Yugoslav People's Army. Around 100,000 would die by the war's end in 1995.

Communism did not disappear after the Cold War. In China, in fact, it thrived. The People's Republic of China had grown into a powerful nation under Mao Zedong and Deng Xiaoping. Its economy was booming by the 1990s. With international investment, it became even more stable. Communist leaders saw no need to change their system. Other world leaders seemed to confirm

All Chinese high school and college students are still required to undergo several weeks of military training.

that opinion when they overlooked human-rights abuses in favor of increasing trade with China. As growth in China inevitably slows, its people will doubtless be looking for deep reforms.

And what about the nuclear threat? In the decade after the Cold War's end, at least 21 attempted thefts were made at Russian nuclear facilities. Both Russia and the U.S. soon committed to preventing the spread of nuclear weapons and technology. A historic summit took place in Moscow between presidents Bill Clinton and Boris Yeltsin in January 1994. Among other things, they agreed to stop targeting nuclear missiles at each other's countries. Further talks and formal treaties related to nukes and chemical weapons were a part of Russian-American relations throughout the rest of the 1990s and into the 2000s. Today, the U.S. and Russia still account for 93 percent of the world's nuclear weapons. An estimated 15,695 existed as of 2015 and were held by 9 countries.

When *nations* have control over nuclear capabilities, that is one thing. But when individual terrorists acquire nukes, that is something else entirely. Once terrorist networks such as al Qaeda and the self-proclaimed Islamic State entered the scene, fears about nuclear security deepened again. The rise of more individualized (yet networked) terrorists has brought much of the rest of the world together in facing a common and increasingly unstable enemy.

No longer is the world pitted East against West. It is one group, one belief system, one financial backer against another. The Cold War may have thawed, but some of the same stumbling blocks and attitudes remain. The combatants are more numerous. They may have differing goals. However, the stakes are just as high. In this era of modern warfare marked by hot and cold terrorist activity, temperatures continue to spike. It is up to each and every nation to learn from the lessons of the not-too-distant past, reassuring one another that this next turning point will be more positive than the last.

POINTING OUT

MUSICAL AMBASSADORS

In December 2014, president Barack Obama made a historic change in U.S. policy toward Cuba. He announced that the two countries would be "normalizing relations." When Obama shook hands with Cuban president Raúl Castro on April 11, 2015, it marked the first time American and Cuban heads of state had met since 1961. The following month, the Minnesota Orchestra flew directly from Minneapolis to Havana for a goodwill tour. For three days, the professional musicians performed concerts and absorbed the joyful welcome from Cuban audiences. Americans listened to the radio broadcasts and expressed hope that such examples of cultural outreach could continue.

Since 1989, artists have painted murals on the remaining sections of the Berlin Wall, and parts of the wall have been featured in exhibitions around the world.

May 8, 1945	Germany surrenders on all fronts to the Allies. Soon the country—including the capital city of Berlin—is divided into four zones.
June 25, 1950	North Korea invades the democratic republic of South Korea.
October 4, 1957	The Soviet Union launches *Sputnik 1*, the first space satellite.
April 17, 1961	Kennedy sends 1,400 Cuban exiles to invade Cuba at the Bay of Pigs, but the invasion fails.
August 13, 1961	The border between East and West Berlin is closed, and the Berlin Wall begins as a fence of barbed wire.
October 1962	During the Cuban Missile Crisis, Kennedy tries to prevent nuclear war after Soviet missile bases are discovered in Cuba.
April 1965	The U.S. commits combat troops to South Vietnam. More than 58,000 will die there over the next decade.
October 6, 1973	An Arab coalition of Egyptian and Syrian forces attacks Israel, starting the Yom Kippur War, or 1973 Arab-Israeli War.
December 25, 1979	The Soviet Union invades Afghanistan to support the communist government; the U.S. provides aid to the resistance fighters.
March 11, 1985	Mikhail Gorbachev becomes the leader of the Soviet Union.
November 4, 1989	Approximately one million demonstrators rally for democracy in East Berlin's main square. Five days later, the Wall starts coming down.
October 3, 1990	West and East Germany are formally reunited as a single country.
July 31, 1991	The U.S. and Soviet Union sign the Strategic Arms Reduction Treaty, which became effective in 1994.
December 25, 1991	The Soviet Union is dissolved, and the Russian Federation is born.

capitalist—describing an economic and political system in which a country's trade and industry are controlled by private owners (rather than the state) for profit

colonial—relating to a colony, an area or country controlled by another country

communist—involving a system of government in which all property and business is owned and controlled by the state, with the goal of creating a classless society

détente—French for "relaxation of tensions," it usually describes a policy or period of calmness between nations

Fidel Castro—political leader of Cuba who came to power in 1959 by overthrowing the government of dictator Fulgencio Batista and remained in power until 2008; under Castro, Cuba became the first communist nation in the Western Hemisphere

infrastructure—physical structures such as bridges, roads, and buildings, plus the facilities needed to power and sustain them

mole—an employee of one intelligence service who actually works for another service or who works undercover within the enemy group in order to gather intelligence

Nikita Khrushchev—leader of the Soviet Union from 1953 to 1964, who sought a policy of "peaceful coexistence" with the U.S.

peninsula—a piece of land sticking out into a body of water and nearly surrounded by that water

repressive—limiting the freedom of a person or group

Soviet Union—the Union of Soviet Socialist Republics, established in 1922, was governed by a single communist party, with Moscow as its capital, until the end of 1991

Strategic Defense Initiative—also known as "Star Wars," this proposed missile defense system was advocated by Ronald Reagan beginning in 1983; in 1993, president Bill Clinton renamed it the Ballistic Missile Defense Organization, but it was never fully deployed for action

Campbell, Geoffrey A. *The Home Front: The Cold War in the United States.* San Diego, Calif.: Lucent Books, 2003.

Institute for Economics & Peace. *Economic Consequences of War on the U.S. Economy.* Washington, D.C.: Institute for Economics & Peace, 2011.

Lebow, Richard Ned, and Janice Gross Stein. *We All Lost the Cold War.* Princeton, N.J.: Princeton University Press, 1994.

Sabato, Larry J. *The Kennedy Half-Century: The Presidency, Assassination, and Lasting Legacy of John F. Kennedy.* New York: Bloomsbury, 2013.

Zubok, Vladislav, and Constantine Pleshakov. *Inside the Kremlin's Cold War: From Stalin to Khrushchev.* Cambridge, Mass.: Harvard University Press, 1996.

CIA Museum Collection

https://www.cia.gov/about-cia/cia-museum/experience-the-collection/index.html
Stories, biographies, and a detailed timeline
of events during the Cold War years.

The Cold War Museum

http://www.coldwar.org/
Quiz yourself with a trivia game and check out online exhibits.

Note: Every effort has been made to ensure that the websites listed above are suitable for children, that they have educational value, and that they contain no inappropriate material. However, because of the nature of the Internet, it is impossible to guarantee that these sites will remain active indefinitely or that their contents will not be altered.